Learning to Dance IN THE RAIN

The Power of Gratitude

Mac Anderson | BJ Gallagher

Gratitude unlocks the fullness of life.

It turns what we have into enough, and more.

It turns denial into acceptance, chaos to order, confusion to clarity.

It can turn a meal into a feast,

a house into a home, a stranger into a friend.

Gratitude makes sense of our past, brings peace for today,

and creates a vision for tomorrow.

MELODY BEATTIE
therapist, author

GRATITUDE

LIFE'S NOT ABOUT
    WAITING FOR THE STORMS TO PASS...
IT'S ABOUT
    LEARNING TO DANCE IN THE RAIN.

The Power of Gratitude

MAC ANDERSON | BJ GALLAGHER

Published by SimpleTruths, LLC
1952 McDowell Road
Naperville, Illinois 60563
800-900-3427
www.simpletruths.com

Design and production: Koechel Peterson & Associates, Inc., Minneapolis, MN

Printed and bound in China.

ISBN 978-1-60810-016-3

01 4CPG 09

TABLE OF CONTENTS

Introduction 6

Dancing in Rain Showers 10

Dancing in Storms 24

Dancing in a Hurricane 40

Nine Dance Lessons for Your Own Life 56

   Begin by being thankful for what *didn't* happen   61

   Plant a "Trouble Tree"   64

   Learn "The Glad Game" and play it often   70

   Practice forgiveness—let go of resentments   74

   Look for the lesson in every experience   81

   Make gratitude a habit   86

   Express your gratitude   90

   Teach others how to be grateful   95

   Create your own future   98

Conclusion 105

About the Authors 109

THE DATE WAS JULY 16, 2008. *It was late in the afternoon, and I was sitting in my hotel room in Louisville, Kentucky. I was scheduled to speak that evening for the Kentucky Association of School Administrators (KASA). I was feeling a little "down in the dumps." I hadn't gotten to exercise lately because of my travel schedule and recently I'd experienced some mild bouts of vertigo (that inner ear condition that can cause the room to start spinning.) You got it…speaking and "spinning" are not good partners!*

My keynote presentation was scheduled for 7:00 P.M., but I had been invited to show up at 6:00 to see a performance they said I'd enjoy. Little did I know that I was about to see something I would never forget.

They introduced the young musician. Welcome…Mr. Patrick Henry Hughes. He was rolled onto the stage in his wheelchair and began to play the piano. His fingers danced across the keys as he made beautiful music.

He then began to sing as he played, and it was even more beautiful. For some reason, however, I knew that I was seeing something special. There was this aura about him that I really can't explain and the smile…his smile was magic!

About ten minutes into Patrick's performance, someone came on the stage and said, "I'd like to share a seven-minute video titled, *The Patrick Henry Hughes story*." Then the lights went dim.

Patrick Henry Hughes was born with no eyes and a tightening of the joints, which left him crippled for life. However, as a child, he was fitted with artificial eyes and placed in a wheelchair. Before his first birthday, he discovered the piano. His mom said, "I could hit any note on the piano, and within one or two tries, he'd get it." By his second birthday, he was playing requests ("You Are My Sunshine," "Twinkle, Twinkle, Little Star"). His father was ecstatic. "We might not play baseball, but we can play music together."

Today, Patrick is a junior at the University of Louisville. His father attends classes with him and he's made nearly all A's, with the exception of 3 B's. He's also a part of the 214-member marching band. You read it right … the marching band! He's a blind, wheelchair-bound trumpet player; and he and his father do it together. They attend all the band practices and the half-time performance in front of thousands. His father rolls and rotates his son around the field to the cheers of Patrick's fans. In order to attend Patrick's classes and every band practice, his father works the graveyard shift at UPS. Patrick says, "My dad's my hero."

But even more than his unbelievable musical talent, it was Patrick's "attitude of gratitude" that touched my soul. On stage, between songs, he talked to the audience about his life and about how blessed he was. He said, "God made me blind and unable to walk. BIG DEAL! He gave me the ability… the musical gifts I have…the great opportunity to meet new people."

When his performance was over, Patrick and his father were on the stage together. The crowd rose to their feet and cheered for over five minutes. It gave me giant goose bumps!

My life was ready to meet Patrick Henry Hughes. I needed a hero, and I found one for the ages. If I live to be a hundred, I'll never forget that night, that smile, that music, but most importantly, that wonderful "attitude of gratitude."

I returned to Chicago and shared Patrick's story with my wife, my friends, and our team at Simple Truths. About two weeks later, I received a letter from a friend. He said, "Mac, I don't know who said it, but I think you'll love this quote."

"Life is not about waiting for the storms to pass…
it's about learning to dance in the rain!"

I thought…*that's it!* We all face adversity in our life. However, it's not the adversity, but how we react to it that will determine the joy and happiness in our lives. During tough times, do we spend too much time feeling sorry for ourselves, or can we, with gratitude…learn how to dance in the rain?

It almost sounds too simple to feel important, but one word…*gratitude*, can change your attitude, and thus your life, forever. Sarah Breathnach said it best…

"When we choose not to focus on what is missing
from our lives but are grateful for the abundance that's present
...we experience heaven on earth."

DANCING

DANCING IN RAIN SHOWERS

As you wander through life, brother,
whatever be your goal,
keep your eye upon the donut,
and not upon the hole.

Sign in the Mayflower Coffee Shop, Chicago

SHOWERS

BRITISH WRITER AND PHILOSOPHER *Mary Wollstonecraft wrote that, "Nothing, I am sure, calls for the faculties so much as being obliged to struggle with the world." Just as our physical muscles are developed by lifting heavy weights and doing resistance training, so, too, our intelligence, personality, and character are developed by engaging with the world—especially dealing with problems, difficulties, and challenges.*

A wise Buddhist master once told me, "When you are considering someone to be your guru or teacher, first go for a ride with him in his car. That will tell you much about whether or not he is the right person for you."

I have thought of that cautionary insight many times when I am the one doing the driving:

Am I patient and calm when driving?

Am I generous in letting other drivers go first?

How do I behave when I'm stuck in gridlock traffic?

Is my driving sensible and safe, or am I reckless behind the wheel?

Am I mindful in each moment, paying full attention to my driving?

Above all, am I *grateful* . . . for my car, which carries me without complaint, for the highways that enable me to travel quickly, for the road maintenance crews who keep my journey smooth and safe, and for the other drivers who are my fellow travelers on Life's journey?

I have to ask myself, "Would anyone choose *me* to be their guru or teacher, based on how I conduct myself behind the wheel?"

I am grateful for the wise lesson.

BJ Gallagher

Can you see the holiness in those things you take for granted—a paved road or a washing machine? If you concentrate on finding what is good in every situation, you will discover that your life will suddenly be filled with gratitude, a feeling that nurtures the soul.

RABBI HAROLD KUSHNER
author of *When Bad Things Happen to Good People*

THE HARDEST ARITHMETIC TO MASTER IS THAT WHICH ENABLES US TO COUNT OUR BLESSINGS.

ERIC HOFFER author of *The True Believer*, Presidential Medal of Freedom winner

I GUESS I'M JUST *lucky*

Chellie Champbell

OOPS! MY CAR BROKE AGAIN. *Well, machinery gets old and stuff happens. This time I was in a parking garage behind a restaurant in Culver City [California]. It was 10:00 P.M., and I was one of the last people leaving a networking dinner. The key wouldn't turn in the ignition, and the steering column was locked. The parking lot attendant came over and tried to get it to work too, but no go. Rats.*

Okay, time to play "The Glad Game." Thank you, God, for the Auto Club. Thank you, God, for cell phones. I made some notes for my book and did some affirmations while I waited for the tow truck. Finally, my knight in shining armor arrived in the person of Bijan, astride his trusty steed, the Auto Club tow truck. He strapped my car to his truck. I got in the cab, and we took off for the repair shop.

"You know, there are some good things about this," Bijan said to me as we drove away. I looked at him in astonishment. The tow truck driver from Iran was playing "The Glad Game"! He continued, "If your wheels hadn't been straight, I wouldn't have been able to tow you."

"Really?" I commented. "I guess I'm just lucky!"

When it comes to life,
the critical thing
is whether you take
things for granted
or take them with
gratitude.

G. K. CHESTERTON
English-born Gabonese novelist,
essayist, critic, and poet

15

"Yes, you are," he agreed. " A lot of things could have made this situation worse than it is."

"Did you ever see the movie *Pollyanna*?" I asked suspiciously.

He shook his head, but told me that the trick to being happy in life is to look at what you do have instead of what you don't have. He said that so many people are always unhappy because they're looking up at the few who have more than they do instead of down at all of those who have less than they do. We had a great philosophical discussion for the entire ride to the auto repair shop. What could have been an unhappy, angry experience was fun instead. I had met a kindred spirit from the other side of the world. And then, although it wasn't part of his job, he drove me home.

I guess I'm just lucky.

*from *The Wealthy Spirit* by Chellie Campbell

LUCKY

I AM *thankful*

FOR A LAWN THAT NEEDS MOWING,

WINDOWS THAT NEED CLEANING,

AND GUTTERS THAT NEED FIXING

BECAUSE IT MEANS I HAVE A HOME....

I AM THANKFUL FOR THE PILES OF

LAUNDRY AND IRONING BECAUSE

IT MEANS MY LOVED ONES ARE NEARBY.

Nancie J. Carmody
author

17

WEATHER *report*

BJ Gallagher

"Any day I'm vertical
is a good day"
. . . that's what I always say.
And I give thanks for my health.

If you ask me,
"How are you?"

I'll answer, "GREAT!"
because in saying so,
I make it so.
And I give thanks
I can choose my attitude.

When Life gives me dark clouds and rain,
I appreciate the moisture
that brings a soft curl to my hair.

When Life gives me sunshine,
     I gratefully turn my face up
     to feel its warmth on my cheeks.

When Life brings fog,
     I hug my sweater around me
     and give thanks for the cool shroud of mystery
     that makes the familiar seem different and intriguing.

When Life brings snow,
     I dash outside to catch the first flakes on my tongue,
     relishing the icy miracle that is a snowflake.

Life's events and experiences
are like the weather—
     they come and go,
     no matter what my preference.

So, what the heck?!
     I might as well decide to enjoy them.

For indeed,
     there IS a time for every purpose
        under Heaven.

And each season brings its own unique blessings…
   and I give thanks.

This is the precious present, regardless of what yesterday was like, regardless of what tomorrow may bring. When your inner eyes open, you can find immense beauty hidden within the inconsequential details of daily life. When your inner ears are open, you can hear the subtle, lovely music of the universe everywhere you go. When the heart of your heart opens, you can take deep pleasure in the company of the people around you—family, friends, acquaintances, or strangers—including those whose characters are less than perfect, just as your character is less than perfect. When you are open to the beauty, mystery, and grandeur of ordinary existence, you "get it" that it always has been beautiful, mysterious, and grand and always will be.

TIMOTHY RAY MILLER
author of *How to Want What You Have*

WHEN I FIRST OPEN MY EYES UPON THE MORNING
MEADOWS AND LOOK OUT UPON THE BEAUTIFUL
WORLD, I THANK GOD I AM ALIVE.

Ralph Waldo Emerson
essayist, philosopher, poet, and leader of the Transcendentalist movement in the early nineteenth century

Gratefulness is the key to a happy life
that we hold in our hands, because
if we are not grateful, then no matter how
much we have, we will not be happy—
because we will always want to have
something else or something more.

BROTHER DAVID STEINDL-RAST
Austrian-born Benedictine spiritual
teacher and author

IF THERE IS A SIN AGAINST THIS *life,* IT CONSISTS PERHAPS NOT SO MUCH IN DESPAIRING OF LIFE AS IN HOPING FOR ANOTHER LIFE AND IN ELUDING THE IMPLACABLE GRANDEUR OF THIS LIFE.

Albert Camus
Algerian-born French author, philosopher, and journalist,
winner of the Nobel Prize in Literature

If the only prayer you say in your whole life is "thank you,"
that would suffice.

MEISTER ECKHART
German theologian, philosopher, and mystic

For today and its blessings, I owe the world an attitude of gratitude.

CLARENCE E. HODGES
minister and author

DANCING IN STORMS

Life will bring you pain all by itself.
Your responsibility is to create joy.

Milton Erickson, M.D., psychiatrist
specializing in medical hypnosis

STORMS

SOMEONE WISE ONCE SAID, *"Circumstances don't determine character—they reveal it." Who we are as human beings is revealed most clearly during times of struggle, hardship, pain, and suffering. It's easy to be a good person when things are going great. But when times get tough, that's when you'll really find out stuff you're made of.*

Nowhere is this more true than with regard to gratitude. Are you grateful when the storm clouds gather, and it rains on your parade? Can you find gratitude in your heart when you don't get what you want? Do you feel grateful when illness strikes, loved ones don't show up for you, jobs and careers disappoint, and nothing seems to be going your way?

Gratitude is not a fair weather virtue. True gratitude means appreciating your life no matter what the storms may bring. Is simply being alive gift enough for you to feel grateful?

YOU HAVE WITHIN YOU RIGHT NOW,
EVERYTHING YOU NEED TO DEAL WITH WHATEVER
THE WORLD CAN THROW AT YOU.

BRIAN TRACY, motivational speaker and author

Life at any time can
become difficult: life at
any time can become easy.
It all depends upon how one
adjusts oneself to life.

MORARJI DESAI
Prime Minister of India

MOST OF US REMEMBER ROY CAMPANELLA. *Certainly, many people in New York do! He was a catcher with the old Brooklyn Dodgers, and he is now in the Hall of Fame. One of the first African Americans to play major league baseball, Roy was on the same team as Jackie Robinson and was as beloved and valuable.*

In the midst of his career, Roy was in an automobile accident that left him a quadriplegic. Most of his rehabilitation work was done at the famous Rusk Institute for Rehabilitative Medicine in New York.

Often, as he wheeled through the corridors of the Rusk Institute, Roy reported, he would stop by a plaque that was mounted on the wall. It contains the words of a poem called "A Creed for Those Who Have Suffered," written by an unknown Confederate soldier:

I asked God for strength, that I might achieve.
I was made weak, that I might learn to humbly obey . . .

I asked for health, that I might do great things.
I was given infirmity, that I might do better things . . .

I asked for riches, that I might be happy.
I was given poverty, that I might be wise . . .

I asked for power, that I might have the praise of men.
I was given weakness, that I might feel the need of God . . .

I asked for all things, that I might enjoy life.
I was given life, that I might enjoy all things . . .

I got nothing I asked for—but everything I had hoped for.

Almost despite myself, my unspoken prayers were answered.
I am, among men, most richly blessed!

Who, among us, is not so richly blessed—with adversity, yet an abundant life of peace and happiness?

When one door closes another door opens;
but we so often look so long and so regretfully upon the closed door,
that we do not see the ones which open for us.

ALEXANDER GRAHAM BELL
scientist, innovator, inventor of the telephone

BLESSED

THOUGH NO ONE CAN GO BACK AND MAKE

A BRAND NEW START, ANYONE CAN START

FROM NOW AND MAKE A BRAND NEW ENDING.

Carl Bard, Scottish theologian, writer, broadcaster

REALITY *show*

BJ Gallagher

I grew up watching
    entirely too much television.

My mind was filled with rosy images:

    Families of beautiful kids
    and wise, patient, perfect parents,

    Love stories that always ended
    with "happily ever after,"

    Dramas in which
    the good guys always win.

All these and more—
    images of Life as it should be.

But then I grew up
    and discovered that Life is a reality show—
        a jumble of comedy, tragedy, pathos and farce—
            not a carefully scripted, smooth performance.

Families aren't always safe and nurturing;
    love stories often end in heartbreak;
      and sometimes,
        the bad guys get away.

How can I accept
        a world of such unfairness?
How am I to come to terms with
        suffering,
                disappointment,
                        and pain?

Can I still feel grateful
        when my heart is heavy?
Can I still give thanks
        when my hopes are dashed
                and my dreams shattered?
Can I appreciate what's good in the world,
        in spite of much that is bad?

Yes, I can,
        for in my chest
                beats a heart of hope.

I have seen the tiny crocus flower
push up through the winter snow—
        a harbinger of beauty and new growth to come.

I have spotted the rainbow on a stormy day—
        a symbol of promise and Providence.

I have witnessed the sunrise—
        just when I thought the darkness would never end.

And I know that love and beauty are all around me,
        if only I will look for them.

As we express our gratitude,
we must never forget that the highest
appreciation is not to utter words,
but to live by them.

JOHN F. KENNEDY
35th President of the U.S.

Become A POSSIBILITARIAN,

NO MATTER HOW DARK THINGS SEEM TO BE,

OR ACTUALLY ARE, RAISE YOUR SIGHTS

AND SEE POSSIBILITIES—ALWAYS SEE THEM

FOR THEY'RE ALWAYS THERE.

Norman Vincent Peale
pastor, author of *The Power of Positive Thinking*

Walk on through the wind,
walk on through the rain,
though your dreams
be tossed and blown.

Walk on, walk on
with hope in your heart
and you'll never walk alone.

You'll never walk alone.

RICHARD RODGERS AND OSCAR HAMMERSTEIN II
composers, lyricists

DEVELOP AN ATTITUDE OF GRATITUDE,

AND GIVE THANKS FOR EVERYTHING THAT

HAPPENS TO YOU, KNOWING THAT EVERY

STEP FORWARD IS A STEP TOWARD

ACHIEVING SOMETHING BIGGER AND

BETTER THAN YOUR CURRENT SITUATION.

Brian Tracy
motivational speaker and author

GRATITUDE

Gratitude bestows reverence,

allowing us to encounter everyday epiphanies,

    those transcendent moments of awe

    that change forever how we experience life and the world.

JOHN MILTON
English poet, historian, scholar, author of *Paradise Lost*

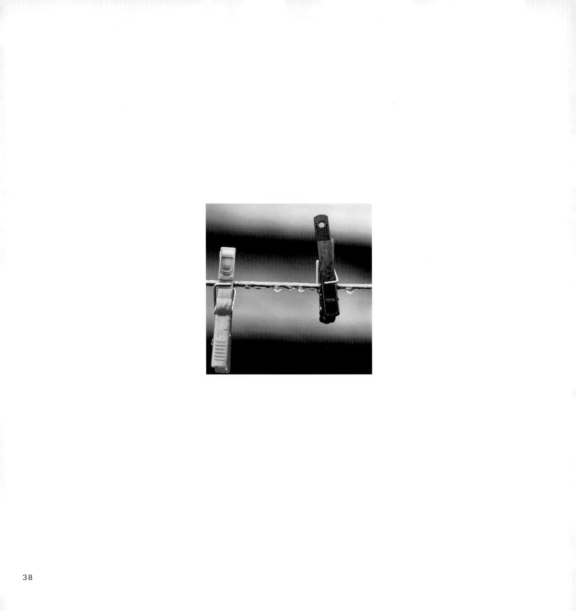

LET US NOT

LOOK BACK IN ANGER,

NOR FORWARD IN FEAR,

BUT AROUND IN AWARENESS.

James Thurber, humorist, cartoonist

DANCING IN A HURRICANE

Buddha said that fortune changes like the swish of a horse's tail.
Tomorrow could be the first day of thirty years of quadriplegia…
The more you open to life, the less death becomes the enemy.
When you start using death as a means of focusing on life,
then everything becomes just as it is, just this moment,
an extraordinary opportunity to be really alive.

Stephen Levine
poet, spiritual teacher, author of *Who Dies?*

HURRICANE

FOR SOME PEOPLE, *Life's difficulties are much more than storms—they are horrific hurricanes. Enormous calamities can happen to anyone at any time—we never know who might be struck by tragedy.*

We are grateful when it isn't us. "Thank God that didn't happen to me," we whisper to ourselves. "I don't know how I would have handled such misfortune."

And we are inspired by the example set by others:

- actor Michael J. Fox and his valiant struggle with Parkinson's disease,

- basketball hero Magic Johnson, living his life with the HIV virus,

- physicist Stephen Hawking, who continues his brilliant scientific work despite being totally crippled by Lou Gehrig's Disease (ALS),

- Senator John McCain, who survived broken bones and years of torture as a North Vietnam prisoner of war,

- Holocaust author Elie Wiesel, who wrote about his search for meaning in the living hell of concentration camps in Nazi Germany,

- blind/deaf Helen Keller, who overcame her disability and went on to teach and inspire millions of others to do the same,

- "Superman" actor Christopher Reeve, determined to overcome his quadriplegia and spinal cord injury caused by falling from a horse.

These people and many like them are amazing human beings—not just because of the suffering they endured—but because they experienced gratitude in the midst of disaster. They were grateful not only to be alive, but grateful to have found meaning and purpose. They became who they were—not in spite of their pain—but because of it.

AN OPTIMIST SEES AN OPPORTUNITY
IN EVERY CALAMITY; A PESSIMIST SEES A
CALAMITY IN EVERY OPPORTUNITY.

WINSTON CHURCHILL, British Prime Minister

GRATITUDE AMONG THE *ashes*

Julie Anna Hill

IT WAS THE YEAR FROM HELL—*September 1993 to September 1994—the dog died, my marriage of 24 years ended, and my house burned down. I had moved into a new rented house with my youngest son, after my husband and I split up. We'd been in the house just six weeks. I went to a dinner party one night, and as I drove home, I saw helicopters hovering in the general vicinity of my new home. Smoke was billowing into the sky, and sirens were wailing. As I got closer, I thought, **Wouldn't it be awful if that was my house?** Then I turned the corner, and sure enough, it was my house.*

I was devastated. It had been such a horrible year, and now everything I owned had gone up in smoke. Mementos, baby pictures, family keepsakes, clothes, furniture—everything was destroyed. My marriage was gone, my dog was gone, my home was gone, and all my worldly possessions, except my car and the clothes on my back, were gone too.

My son and I stayed with a friend for a couple of nights. Then my friend Gail heard about the fire, called me up, and said, "Come move into my house. I have seven bedrooms and five bathrooms—plenty of space for you and your son." It was a sprawling ranch house on a double lot in La Jolla, with an ocean view, to boot. Gail had three kids at home, but there was still plenty of room for me and my son, Sutton. Her offer was a godsend. Little did I know that her offer of a temporary place to stay would turn into a living arrangement that lasted two and a half years.

Gail and I had a lot in common. We had both been raised Catholic and our unconscious minds had been programmed the same way—we saw ourselves as good little Catholic girls who were gonna stay married forever. But both of our husbands decided they didn't want to be married anymore, and

45

CLARITY

so here we were, two single mothers, dazed, confused, and in a fog. We had followed the rules . . . why were we not happy? Gail and I spent the next couple of years sorting out a lot of things together.

After we moved in, I soon began to look for a permanent place to live. After a few weeks, Gail said, "Please don't leave. I've never had so much freedom!" Having me in the house meant someone to help take care of her kids, someone to share cooking and gardening, and someone to share day-to-day life. She loved having me there, and I loved being there. So we stayed.

It was an important chapter in my life. Gail and I gardened together, talking back and forth as we worked in the soil. We both needed time to heal from our divorces, time to sort out the confusion, time to get some clarity on the past and some focus on the future. It was a time of deeper insight and spiritual growth for both of us. Over time, I grew to realize how strong

I really was, how even-tempered, and how I really could get my act together and go on with my life.

Gail's generosity was more than anyone could ever ask or expect from a friend. She gave me a safe haven in which to mourn and heal and grow into the next chapter of my life. She showed her love in countless ways. I am eternally grateful to have a friend like Gail.

I'm also grateful for the lessons I learned from the fire and the other losses that came so suddenly, so fast. Much to my surprise, I found gratitude among the ashes. I was tested sorely—literally trial by fire. But, like a phoenix, I rose from the ashes strong and whole. I would not be the person I am today if not for that Year from Hell.

*adapted from *Friends Are Everything*, by BJ Gallagher

Gratitude changes
the pangs of memory
to a tranquil joy.

DIETRICH BONHOEFFER
German Lutheran theologian and pastor

THE PILGRIMS MADE SEVEN TIMES MORE GRAVES
THAN HUTS. NO AMERICANS HAVE BEEN MORE
IMPOVERISHED THAN THESE WHO, NEVERTHELESS,
SET ASIDE A DAY OF THANKSGIVING.

H. U. Westermayer, inspirational author

Bless a thing and it will bless you.
Curse it and it will curse you....
If you bless a situation, it has no power to hurt you,
and even if it is troublesome for a time,
it will gradually fade out, if you sincerely bless it.

EMMET FOX

Irish-born American New Thought spiritual leader, author of *The Sermon on the Mount*

THE unthinkable

BJ Gallagher

Disaster strikes.
 The unthinkable occurs.
  Horrible things happen.
   Unspeakable loss rips my heart to shreds.

I don't think I can bear it.
 How can I go on?

I've been told that
God doesn't give you
more than you can handle.

But I don't think that's true.

God often gives me more than I can handle . . .
 so I'll have to turn to Him for help.

And that which doesn't kill me
 makes my faith stronger.

Gratitude is the sign of noble souls.

AESOP
ancient Greek author of fables

I HAVE LEARNED THAT SOME OF THE NICEST

PEOPLE YOU'LL EVER MEET ARE THOSE

WHO HAVE SUFFERED A TRAUMATIC EVENT OR LOSS.

I ADMIRE THEM FOR THEIR STRENGTH,

BUT MOST ESPECIALLY FOR THEIR LIFE GRATITUDE—

A GIFT OFTEN TAKEN FOR GRANTED BY THE

AVERAGE PERSON IN SOCIETY.

Sasha Azevedo
actress, athlete, model

STRENGTH

Gratitude is our most direct line to God and the angels.

If we take the time, no matter how crazy and troubled we feel,

we can find something to be thankful for.

The more we seek gratitude, the more reason the angels will give us

for gratitude and joy to exist in our lives.

TERRY LYNN TAYLOR

author of *Messengers of Light* and other books on angels and the Divine

There is often in people
to whom "the worst" has happened
an almost transcendent freedom,
for they have faced "the worst"
and survived it.

CAROL PEARSON
speaker and author of *The Hero Within*

GRATITUDE IS NOT ONLY THE GREATEST OF ALL
VIRTUES, BUT THE PARENT OF ALL OTHERS.

Marcus Tullius Cicero
Roman statesman, lawyer, political theorist, and philosopher,
generally perceived as one of the most versatile minds of ancient Rome

DANCE LESSONS

The essence of all beautiful art,
all great art, is gratitude.

Friedrich Nietzsche,
German classical scholar, philosopher, and cultural critic

LESSONS

NINE DANCE LESSONS FOR
your own life

READING INSPIRATIONAL STORIES *about the trials and tribulations of others is one thing—finding gratitude in your own struggles and suffering is quite another. It's easy to appreciate and applaud the courage of others who've transcended their pain to find beauty and meaning—but it can be much harder when it's our turn to transcend.*

What can we learn from others' experiences? How can we adapt their lessons to our own lives?

The following nine tips might be considered "dance lessons" for the storms that will, sooner or later, blow into your life. If other people have learned to dance in the rain, so can you.

Begin by being thankful for what *didn't* happen.
Plant a "Trouble Tree."
Learn "The Glad Game" and play it often.
Practice forgiveness—let go of resentments.
Look for the lesson in every experience.
Make gratitude a habit.
Express your gratitude.
Teach others how to be grateful.
Create your own future.

Dancing in the rain isn't something that most of us are born knowing how to do. We learn it. We learn it from others; we learn it from Life. The more we dance, the better we get at it. With practice, dancing in the rain becomes almost automatic. We no longer seek to run from storms...instead, we toss back our heads, throw out our arms, pick up our feet, and DANCE!

BEGIN BY BEING THANKFUL FOR WHAT *DIDN'T* happen

IF PRACTICING AN ATTITUDE OF GRATITUDE *during Life's storms is a bit much for you to handle right now, that's okay. When things are tough, most people have a hard time being thankful. They're so caught up in what's wrong in the present moment that they simply can't see some things are still right.*

If that's true for you, then accept it. You're going through a rough patch, and you don't like it one bit. Very normal, very human.

But now ask yourself this: Could it be worse? Are there bad things that could have happened but didn't? Are there other people who are suffering from worse calamities than yours? Are you glad that the mess you're in isn't worse?

If your answer is yes, then there's something to be grateful for. It may be only a small comfort right now, but it's a start.

Make a list of some of the terrible things that *didn't* happen. For example:

> You lost your job...but you didn't lose your health.
>
> The bank foreclosed on your house...but your family didn't desert you.
>
> Your dog died...but your spouse didn't.

THANKFUL

Your mother has Alzheimer's disease... but your father doesn't.

You were in a car accident... but you weren't seriously hurt.

You broke your leg... but you didn't break your neck.

You're suffering from depression... but you don't have cancer.

You're broke... but you're not homeless.

Your house flooded... but your family photo albums were
undamaged.

No matter how bad things are, they could always be worse. Start finding gratitude for what might have happened, but didn't.

You may not be thankful for *everything*—but you can always be thankful for *something*.

Let us rise up and be thankful,

for if we didn't learn a lot today, at least we learned a little;

and if we didn't learn a little, at least we didn't get sick;

and if we got sick, at least we didn't die;

so, let us all be thankful.

PLANT A "*trouble tree*"

BJ Gallagher

WE ALL HAVE STORMS COME *through our lives, but one thing is for sure—we have no right to make everyone else miserable with our own unhappiness. No need to rain on others' parades. A simple story illustrates my point:*

The Trouble Tree

The carpenter I hired to help me restore an old farmhouse had just finished a rough first day on the job. A flat tire made him lose an hour of work, his electric saw quit, and now his ancient pickup truck refused to start.

While I drove him home, he sat in stony silence.

On arriving, he invited me in to meet his family. As we walked toward the front door, he paused briefly at a small tree, touching tips of the branches with both hands.

When opening the door, he underwent an amazing transformation. His tanned face was wreathed in smiles, and he hugged his two small children and gave his wife a kiss.

Afterward he walked me to the car. We passed the tree, and my curiosity got the better of me. I asked him about what I had seen him do earlier.

"Oh, that's my trouble tree," he replied. "I know I can't help having troubles on the job, but one thing's for sure, troubles don't belong in the house with my wife and the children. So I just hang them up on the tree every night when I come home. Then in the morning I pick them up again.

"Funny thing is," he smiled, "when I come out in the morning to pick 'em up, there ain't nearly as many as I remember hanging up the night before."

I don't know who first told this story—no one seems to know—but he or she must have been a very wise person. Putting boundaries around our problems is a really good idea—it prevents our difficulties from spilling over onto other people (especially loved ones), who can't do anything about our problems. Why burden them if they can't help us?

So, plant yourself a trouble tree outside your front door—or a potted trouble plant, if you live in an apartment—and use it whenever you come home.

Be grateful that you have loved ones to go home to, even if your loved one is simply your beloved dog or cherished cat or prized goldfish.

And when you pick up your troubles on the way out each morning, be grateful that they're not as heavy as they were the night before.

REJOICE IN THE THINGS THAT ARE PRESENT;
ALL ELSE IS BEYOND THEE.

MONTAIGNE, French Renaissance scholar and influential essayist

"The Glad Game"

IN HER WONDERFUL BOOK, *The Wealthy Spirit*, *Chellie Campbell describes how, when she was a girl, her mother taught her to play "The Glad Game." On days when Chellie came home from school complaining about something—a bully on the playground, a harsh teacher, a skinned knee, or difficult homework—Chellie's mom would hug her, kiss away her tears, and then suggest, "Okay, enough complaining. Let's play 'The Glad Game.'"*

"The Glad Game" is another name for a Gratitude List. "The Glad Game" helps you focus on what's *right* in your world today, instead of what's wrong. Chellie's mom was a very wise woman, teaching her that no matter what your troubles, there are still plenty of things to be grateful for: a sunny day, good food to eat, a loving family, a house to live in, a family pet to love, a handful of friends to enjoy, and much, much more.

Chellie would follow her mother's suggestion:

"I'm glad I have you as my mom."
"I'm glad the weekend is almost here."
"I'm glad I have some nice clothes to wear to school."
"I'm glad I don't have to share my room with my sister anymore."
"I'm glad I get to watch TV when I finish my homework."
"I'm glad we have pie for dessert."

Playing "The Glad Game" is a terrific way to change your attitude in a hurry. We all slip into self-pity once in a while—after all, we're only human. The important thing is to cut the pity-party short and shift into gratitude. An attitude of gratitude will get you much farther in life than complaining and self-pity. Try it and see.

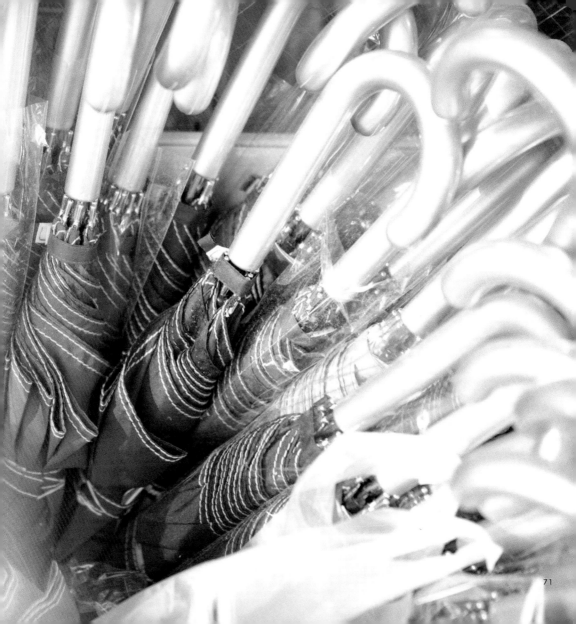

The longer I live, the more I realize
the impact of attitude on life.
Attitude to me is more important than facts.
It is more important than the past, than education,
than money, than circumstances, than failures,
than success, than what other people think or say or do.
It is more important than appearance, gift, or skill.
It will make or break a company . . . a church . . . a home.
The remarkable thing is we have a choice every day
regarding the attitude we will embrace for that day.
We cannot change our past . . .
The only thing we can do is play on the string we have,
and that is our attitude. I am convinced that life is 10%
what happens to me and 90% how I react to it.
And so it is with you . . . we are in charge
of our attitudes.

CHARLES SWINDOLL
pastor, author

PRACTICE *forgiveness—*
LET GO OF RESENTMENTS

SOMEONE WISE ONCE SAID, *"Holding onto a resentment is like swallowing poison, and hoping the other person will die."* Resentment doesn't hurt the person you're angry at—it hurts **you**.

You can't feel resentment and gratitude at the same time. One will always drive out the other. So the question is: Which would you rather be—angry or happy? Indignant or grateful? Upset or serene? Would you rather hold onto your self-righteous resentment or fill your heart with forgiveness and gratitude?

My friend BJ Gallagher told me a great story recently, about her own experience with resentment. She once worked as the training manager for a large metropolitan newspaper, where she found the corporate culture extremely frustrating. The company was a hundred years old, steeped in tradition, and calcified with bureaucracy. Their past success had blinded them to the need for change, and they resisted new ideas with "this is the way we've always done it."

As the years went by, BJ grew more frustrated with their bureaucratic short-sightedness and their inability to embrace the brave new world of the Internet and other global changes. Finally, after butting heads with several senior executives one-too-many times, she left the company.

Reflect upon your
present blessings,
of which every man
has plenty;
not on your past
misfortunes, of which
all men have some.

CHARLES DICKENS
*Victorian English novelist
and social campaigner*

FEELING

But she found that she hadn't left her resentment, frustration, and anger behind when she resigned. She carried them with her, like "rocks in my stomach," she says.

"Weighing me down, always there in my gut."

"I finally decided to write about my experiences and my feelings at the newspaper. I figured it would be a good mental health exercise, purging myself of the negative baggage. I wanted to be rid of that company and those people, once and for all.

"So I wrote and I wrote, enlisting a good friend, Warren Schmidt, to help me in the purging process. It wasn't just a story that poured out—it was a whole book! We called it *A Peacock in the Land of Penguins*. I was the peacock and those newspaper executives were the penguins.

"My resentment fueled my writing. I was gonna show them! I would write my book; it would be wildly successful; and the whole world would know how stupid those penguins were! Today, I shudder to think how my resentfulness poisoned me. I wasn't just resentful—I was vengeful."

"What happened when the book came out?" I asked BJ.

"Not much," she replied. "The newspaper kept doing what it had always done, and I continued my emotional turmoil. My feelings didn't bother the penguins one bit, but those feelings were sure taking a toll on me.

"It took me several more years to finally get over my negative emotions. Through a lot of soul-searching and reflection, I *finally* was able to let go of my resentment. I came to see that there was nothing personal in the way they treated me—they were good people doing what they thought best for

FORGIVE

the company. I was the one who had made it personal. I thought they were making my life miserable on purpose.

"Finally, the time came when I decided to make amends for the harsh, angry things I had said about the company. I invited my former boss to dinner and made my apology. I called the publisher and told him I was sorry for being so resentful. I wrote a letter to another key executive, reiterating my apology. It was a great healing process for me. I *finally* felt free of the resentment that had been eating me up."

"What was the final outcome?" I asked her.

"Gratitude," she replied. "Not only wasn't I resentful anymore, I was grateful to the company. If I hadn't had those painful experiences, I never would

have written a book. And the book became hugely successful—now published in 21 languages—it transformed my business.

"In short, my resentment gave way to gratitude," she smiled. "I owe the penguins a debt of thanks—for giving me such a great tale to tell."

Trading resentments for gratitude isn't always easy, as BJ's story illustrates. It can take a long time and a lot of reflection to be able to see the situation with some emotional maturity.

But it's worth it. For gratitude is a far happier feeling than resentment. Just ask my peacock friend BJ.

LOOK FOR THE LESSON
IN EVERY
experience

BJ Gallagher

SOME MONTHS AGO, *I took my buddy Michael to lunch to cheer him up. Over burgers and beer he was lamenting the end of his latest love affair. He expressed his disappointment in a way that made me laugh, saying: "I guess experience is what you get when you don't get what you want."*

"That's true," I chuckled. "But experience isn't much use unless you learn something from it."

"Yeah," Michael agreed ruefully. "I guess I did learn a few things from this relationship. Mostly, I learned stuff about me. This isn't the first time that a relationship has ended badly for me—in fact, it seems to happen over and over again."

"What do all those relationships have in common?" I asked him.

"Me," he replied glumly.

His response was so morose, we both laughed.

"The problem is not with the women—the problem is with me," Michael explained. "I'm the one who picks 'em."

"And why do you pick the ones you pick?" I queried.

"I like to be the hero," he answered. "I seem to be attracted to broken women, women with problems, women who need saving. Then I get to ride in on my white horse and save them."

"And then what happens?" I prodded.

"I spend a lot of time, energy, and money saving them, only to find that they're still messed up. They don't really want to be saved. They're attached to their suffering, their drama, their complaints," he explained. "I keep thinking that if I make their lives wonderful, then they'll love me for it, and make my life wonderful in return. But it never turns out that way. I make this huge effort to save them, but they don't turn into the women I think they can be—and they certainly don't love me."

"And so what's the lesson?" I asked.

HEALTHY

"The lesson is: I need to feel like a hero in my own life. I need to stop picking broken women just so I can feel good about myself. I shouldn't need a damsel in distress to feel like a hero—I want to learn to pick a woman who is strong and healthy in her own right," he answered. "Then nobody has to save anybody—we just have a great life together."

"Great lesson," I commented. "Something to be grateful for, I suppose."

"Yes, I am grateful," he replied. "I'm grateful I didn't have to go through another marriage and divorce to get the lesson. I've already done that—don't need to do that again."

"I've heard it said that life keeps giving us more opportunities to learn the lessons we need to learn, until we get it right," I mused.

"Then we can move on."

CHOICE

"I'm ready," Michael announced as he finished his beer. "Lesson learned. I'm ready for what's next."

We laughed again; I picked up the check and we left the restaurant.

Michael's story has a happy ending, I'm pleased to report—he DID learn the lesson from his painful experience. Not too long after our lunch conversation, I ran into Michael at the gym.

"Hey, how's it going?" I asked him.

"Great!" he beamed. "I've got a new girlfriend, and she's terrific. Not someone I would have thought of as 'my type' in the past—but I see now that she's perfect for me."

"Wonderful!" I congratulated him.

"Yeah, it's pretty great," he said happily. "I guess that last painful relationship I had taught me what I needed to learn. I'm grateful for the lesson . . . but I'm even more grateful that it's over!"

BE MISERABLE OR MOTIVATE YOURSELF.
WHATEVER HAS TO BE DONE, IT'S ALWAYS
YOUR CHOICE.

Wayne Dyer
motivational speaker and author

MAKE *gratitude* A HABIT

BEHAVIORAL SCIENTISTS TELL US *that if we do something consistently for 21 days, it becomes a habit. That's good news if you're interested in bringing more gratitude into your life. Here are some simple ways to build your gratitude muscles:*

- Before you go to bed at night, write down three things that you're grateful for. Don't make them the obvious things, such as your family or your home or your pets. Look deeper; look for more subtle things that you may be taking for granted.

- On your way to work, notice three to five things that you're grateful for along the way.

- When you're at work, notice a few things about your job, your boss, your coworkers, or your company that you appreciate.

- When you're out running errands or doing chores, see if you can find gratitude for one or two things in the process.

- When you're doing something you don't like to do, see if you can find at least one thing to be grateful for in the process.

These don't have to be big things—little things will do just fine. The more you start to train your mind to look for what's right—rather than what's wrong—the more gratitude you'll feel throughout the day.

Do this for 21 days and see if it doesn't make a difference in your daily life. Keep it up, and a lifetime of gratitude can be yours—no matter what.

When I started counting my blessings,

my whole life turned around.

WILLIE NELSON
country singer

EXPRESS YOUR *gratitude*

KEN BLANCHARD, CO-AUTHOR OF *The One-Minute Manager, teaches his seminar participants to "catch people doing something right…and acknowledge them for it." Appreciation and acknowledgment are so powerful, and yet few people understand that.*

"Thank you" are two of the most powerful words in the English language, but they may very well be the most under-utilized.

We are quick to complain, but slow to compliment. We don't hesitate to point out what's wrong, but completely neglect to point out what's right. We're eager to find fault, but reluctant to praise. We lament our woes, but overlook our blessings.

Esther and Jerry Hicks, in their book, *Ask and It Is Given*, write:

> A desire to *appreciate* is a very good first step; and then as you find more things that you would like to feel appreciation for, it quickly gains momentum. And as you want to feel appreciation, you *attract* something to *appreciate*. And as you *appreciate* it, then you attract something else to appreciate, until, in time, you are experiencing a *Rampage of Appreciation*.

EXPRESSION

Don't you just love that image?…a *Rampage of Appreciation!* Expressing our gratitude brings us more things to be grateful for.

No matter what's going on around you, look for things to appreciate, and then express your appreciation. Express it to other people and express it to God.

If you want more to be grateful for, start by being more grateful.

Feeling gratitude and not expressing it

is like wrapping a present and not giving it.

WILLIAM A. WARD
pastor, author, and teacher

TEACH OTHERS HOW TO BE *grateful*

GRATITUDE IS CONTAGIOUS—*you can catch it from other people and/or they can catch it from you. But you don't spread gratitude by preaching or scolding or admonishing—you spread it by living it. For, as Gandhi wisely said, "We must BE the change we wish to see in the world."*

A simple story illustrates my point:

> According to legend, a young man, while roaming the desert, came across a spring of delicious crystal-clear water. The water was so sweet he filled his leather canteen so he could bring some back to a tribal elder who had been his teacher. After a four-day journey, he presented the water to the old man who took a deep drink, smiled warmly, and thanked his student lavishly for the sweet water. The young man returned to his village with a happy heart.
>
> Later, the teacher let another student taste the water. He spat it out, saying it was awful. It apparently had become stale because of the old leather container. The student challenged his teacher: "Master, the water was foul. Why did you pretend to like it?"
>
> The teacher replied, "You only tasted the water. I tasted the gift. The water was simply the container for an act of loving-kindness and nothing could be sweeter. Heartfelt gifts deserve the return gift of gratitude.
>
> (*Gifts from the Heart* by Michael Josephson)

You teach gratitude to others by living it—every moment, every hour, every day. Others will see the happiness that gratitude brings, and soon, they, too will be grateful. And before you know it, you have started an epidemic of gratitude—what could be more wonderful!

TO SPEAK *gratitude* IS COURTEOUS

AND PLEASANT, TO ENACT GRATITUDE

IS GENEROUS AND NOBLE, BUT TO LIVE

GRATITUDE IS TO TOUCH HEAVEN.

Johannes A. Gaertner, German-born poet, theologian and professor of art history

CREATE YOUR OWN *future*

SPEAKER AND AUTHOR, TOM FELTENSTEIN *often asks people, "Have you ever noticed how Life has endless ways of giving you more of what you don't want?"*

His question makes people chuckle, but he's dead serious when he asks it. The problem is not Life, you see—the problem is us. Many of us are paying so much attention to what we *don't* want, that we actually make things worse. By focusing on what's wrong, we reinforce it, and attract more of the same.

It is an age-old truism that "we become what we think about." Jesus said so; spiritual teachers, wise philosophers, and psychologists all say so. There is ample proof all around us. By putting so much energy into thinking about our problems, we make our lives more problematic.

It's especially important to keep this fact in mind during stormy, difficult times. When you're going through a rough patch, it's only natural to think about the struggle you're having, while overlooking things in your life to be grateful for.

But if you want a bright future, it's *essential* that you think about bright things—and nothing could be brighter than gratitude. You and I create our own futures by the things we think about and appreciate:

- If you want more love in your life, be grateful for the love you already have.

- If you want more money, appreciate the money you have now.

- If you want better health, love and appreciate your body.

- If you want more friends, take really good care of the friends you have now.

- If you want success, be grateful for your past and present successes.

Create your own future through the amazing power of gratitude!

APPRECIATE

FEELING GRATEFUL OR APPRECIATIVE
OF SOMEONE OR SOMETHING IN YOUR
LIFE ACTUALLY ATTRACTS MORE OF
THE THINGS THAT YOU APPRECIATE AND
VALUE INTO YOUR LIFE.

Christiane Northrup, M.D.
women's health and wellness expert

ENJOY

GRATITUDE COMES EASY *when things are going good in our lives—when we enjoy our work, our health is good, we've got enough money to pay our bills, there's food in the kitchen and a roof over our heads. **Of course** we feel grateful when our families are fine and our friendships strong.*

But what happens when things in our lives go awry? For many people, gratitude goes right out the window when Life doesn't show up the way they want it to. Instead of gratitude, they feel disappointment, fear, anger, resentment, shock, anxiety, and/or hopelessness.

Sometimes their faith is shaken by the loss of a loved one, a big career disappointment, or the end of a cherished relationship. "How can God let these bad things happen?" they lament. "Life isn't fair!" they wail. "Why do bad things happen to good people?" they ask.

These feelings are normal human reactions—everyone has felt them at one time or other. And perhaps YOU were feeling some of these feelings when you picked up this book.

We hope that the wisdom and insight shared in the previous pages has helped you find gratitude in the midst of your own struggles, disappointments, and sadness. Our goal has been to share stories and anecdotes from others, so that you might benefit from their experience, strength, and hope. Perhaps Williams Arthur Ward summarized it best:

> The pessimist complains about the wind;
> the optimist expects it to change;
> the realist adjusts the sails.

Being grateful no matter what is going on around you puts you in position to keep your life moving forward, in the best direction possible, given your current circumstances.

There is no way to avoid Life's storms—they come and go whether we want them or not. The best thing each of us can do is learn how to dance in the rain!

FAITH

BJ GALLAGHER *is an inspirational author, speaker, and storyteller. Her books, keynote speeches, and workshops are designed to educate, entertain, and enlighten people—consistently focusing on the "power of positive **doing**."*

She has written twenty-one books, including an international best-seller, *A Peacock in the Land of Penguins*, now published in 21 languages worldwide. Her other books include:

- *YES Lives in the Land of NO: A Tale of Triumph Over Negativity*
- *A True Friend . . . Is Someone Just Like You*
- *What Would Buddha Do at Work?*
- *Everything I Need to Know I Learned from Other Women*

BJ is a much-in-demand keynote speaker, making frequent presentations at conferences and professional gatherings in the United States, Asia, Europe, and Latin America. Her lively presentations inspire and instruct audiences of all types—with a style that is upbeat, fast-paced, funny, dynamic, and charismatic.

Her impressive client list includes: IBM, Chrysler Corporation, Chevron, Southern California Edison, *Los Angeles Times*, Phoenix Newspapers Inc., American Press Institute, *Atlanta Journal-Constitution*, Raytheon, John Deere Credit, TRW, Farm Credit Services of America, U.S. Department of Interior, the American Lung Association, Marathon Realty (Canada), and many others.

To find out more about BJ, her books, and her speaking topics, visit her at: www.bjgallagher.com or www.yeslivesinthelandofno.com

MAC ANDERSON *is the founder of Simple Truths and Successories, Inc., the leader in designing and marketing products for motivation and recognition. These companies, however, are not the first success stories for Mac. He was also the founder and CEO of McCord Travel, the largest travel company in the Midwest, and part owner/VP of sales and marketing for Orval Kent Food Company, the country's largest manufacturer of prepared salads.*

His accomplishments in these unrelated industries provide some insight into his passion and leadership skills. He also brings the same passion to his speaking where he speaks to many corporate audiences on a variety of topics, including leadership, motivation, and team building.

Mac has authored or co-authored twelve books that have sold over three million copies. His titles include:

- *Charging the Human Battery*
- *Motivational Quotes*
- *You Can't Send a Duck to Eagle School*
- *Change is Good … You Go First*
- *The Power of Attitude*
- *To a Child, Love is Spelled T-I-M-E*

- *Customer Love*
- *Finding Joy*
- *212°: The Extra Degree*
- *The Nature of Success*
- *The Essence of Leadership*
- *The Dash*

For more information about Mac, visit www.simpletruths.com

The
simple truths®
DIFFERENCE

For more information, please visit us at:
www.simpletruths.com

Our products are **not available in bookstores ... only direct.**
Therefore, when you purchase a gift from Simple Truths
you're giving something that can't be found elsewhere!

If you have enjoyed this book we invite you to check out our entire
collection of gift books, with free inspirational movies, at
www.simpletruths.com.

You'll discover it's a great way to inspire **friends** and **family,**
or to thank your best **customers** and **employees.**

We would love to hear how Simple Truths books enrich your
life and others around you. Please send your comments to:

Simple Truths Feedback
1952 McDowell Road, Suite 205
Naperville, IL 60563
Or e-mails us at: comments@simpletruths.com

Or call us toll free…
800-900-3427